SCHOLASTIC ENGLISH SKILLS

Handwriting
Workbook

Ages 7–9

SCHOLASTIC ENGLISH SKILLS

Handwriting

Book End, Range Road, Witney, Oxfordshire, OX29 0YD
www.scholastic.co.uk

© 2015, Scholastic Ltd

2 3 4 5 6 7 8 9   6 7 8 9 0 1 2 3 4

British Library Cataloguing-in-Publication Data
A catalogue record for this book is available from the British Library.

ISBN 978-14171-8
Printed by Ashford Colour Press

Due to the nature of the web we cannot guarantee the content or links of any site mentioned. We strongly recommend that teachers check websites before using them in the classroom.

Every effort has been made to trace copyright holders for the works reproduced in this book, and the publishers apologise for any inadvertent omissions.

Author
Christine Moorcroft

Editorial
Rachel Morgan, Anna Hall, Tracy Kewley, Red Door Media

Cover and Series Design
Nicolle Thomas and Neil Salt

Series consultant
Amanda McLeod

Design
Anna Oliwa

Illustration
Joelle Dreidemy

Cover Illustration
Eddie Rego

Lenny illustration
Paul Hutchinson

Contents

How to use this book

- *Scholastic English Skills Workbooks* help your child to practise and improve their skills in English.

- The content is divided into topics. Find out what your child is doing in school, and dip into the practice activities as required.

- Keep the working time short, and come back to an activity if your child finds it too difficult. Ask your child to note any areas of difficulty. Don't worry if your child does not 'get' a concept first time, as children learn at different rates and content is likely to be covered at different times throughout the school year.

- Find out more information about handwriting and check your child's answers at www.scholastic.co.uk/ses/handwriting.

- Give lots of encouragement, complete the 'How did you do' for each activity and the progress chart as your child finishes each chapter.

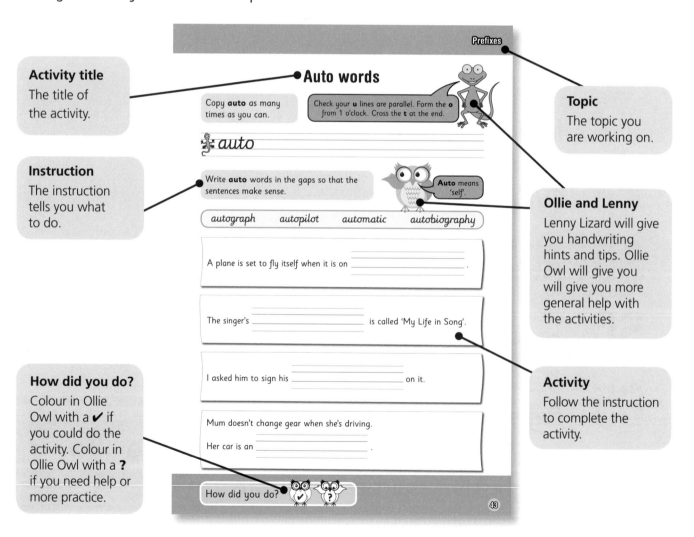

Activity title
The title of the activity.

Instruction
The instruction tells you what to do.

How did you do?
Colour in Ollie Owl with a ✔ if you could do the activity. Colour in Ollie Owl with a **?** if you need help or more practice.

Prefixes

Auto words

Copy **auto** as many times as you can.

Check your **u** lines are parallel. Form the **o** from 1 o'clock. Cross the **t** at the end.

auto

Write **auto** words in the gaps so that the sentences make sense.

Auto means 'self'.

autograph   autopilot   automatic   autobiography

A plane is set to fly itself when it is on _____ .

The singer's _____ is called 'My Life in Song'.

I asked him to sign his _____ on it.

Mum doesn't change gear when she's driving.
Her car is an _____ .

How did you do?

43

Topic
The topic you are working on.

Ollie and Lenny
Lenny Lizard will give you handwriting hints and tips. Ollie Owl will give you will give you more general help with the activities.

Activity
Follow the instruction to complete the activity.

If you need help, ask an adult!

Size

Lenny Lizard appears on tramlines to support letter formation. His 'head', 'body' and 'tail' act as reminders for letter size.

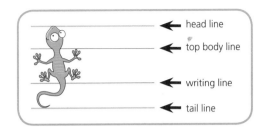

Shape names

Letters are grouped into different shapes, as described below.

- Straight down letters (i, j, l, t, u, y) – start with a 'straight down' stroke.

- Down, up and over letters (b, h, k, m, n, p, r) – start with drawing down, back-up along the same line and then arching over to the right.

- Up, backwards and around letters (a, c, d, e, f, g, o, q, s) – start at 1 o'clock and go up, backwards and around.

- Zooming letters (v, w, x, z) – start with straight zig-zagged lines.

End positions

Letters can end in two positions.

- End-low letters (a, b, c, d, e, f, g, h, i, j, k, l, m, n, p, q, s, t, u, x, y, z) – end on or below the writing line.

- End-high letters (o, r, v, w) – end on the top body line.

Joins

Joining is taking your pen from the end of one letter to the start of the next. There are three different main types of join:

- Diagonal joins – from the end of a letter, diagonally up to the next letter. Formed with end-low or end-high letters.

- Drop-on joins – from the end of a letter, dropping onto an up, backwards and around shape (take your pen over to one o'clock). Formed with end-low or end-high letters.

- Horizontal joins (o, r, v, w) – from the end of a letter, straight across to the next letter. Formed with end-high letters.

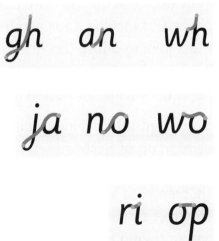

Handedness

This series supports right-handed and left-handed children. We suggest that left-handers adopt a slightly italic style of script, so that it is more comfortable when writing down, up and over letters, and up, backwards and around letters. Teaching left-handers how to sit, position the paper and form letters correctly, should negate any problems.

Sit left-handers to the left of right-handers, or next to another left-hander. This will ensure their elbows don't bump together.

For more information about this series and exercises you can do to support your child's writing development, please see the website www.scholastic.co.uk/ses/handwriting.

- Right-handed alphabet

- Left-handed alphabet

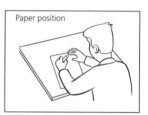

- Right-handed pen grip and paper position

| Dynamic tripod | Paper position |

- Left-handed pen grip and paper position

| Left-handed grip | Paper position |

Joining

This series encourages children to begin joining from Reception, but only when each individual is ready. Children believe joining is difficult; it is not. Joining is the simple process of moving your pen from where one letter ends to where the next one starts. Most joining difficulties are removed if children are told to 'move from the end of that letter to the start of the next'. Using the terminology above helps to identify the start point and height of each letter (Lenny's body, shape names, ending positions and joins).

Do not introduce joining until letter formation is secure; incorrect formation hinders the acquisition of legibility, especially at speed. To judge this, it is important to see a child actually writing, as, once written, it is hard to ascertain how a letter was formed. Some children with weaker visual perception and motor skills may not be able to join, but all effort should be given towards building up this perceptual and motor strength first, before taking that decision (refer to the website for exercises).

Note that the average copying speed for children aged seven is fifty-four letters per minute; fifty-seven letters per minute for children aged eight; and sixty-four letters per minute for children aged nine.

End-low diagonal joins

Make your exit stroke smooth. Go from the end of the letter to the start of the next.

Copy **au** six times.

 *au*

Now write this word four times.

If you don't know what an auk is, look it up in a dictionary!

 auk

Copy each word neatly as many times as it fits along the line. Leave spaces between the words.

 *Paul*

 *autumn*

 *aunt*

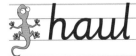 *haul*

How did you do?

End-low diagonal joins

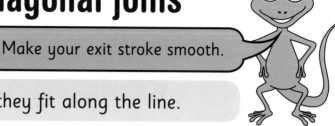

Make your exit stroke smooth.

Copy the letters as many times as they fit along the line.

ch

nk

mp

bl

Copy each word once.

chip	chum	chin	chill	limp	lump	chump	chimp
sink	bunk	pink	punk	blip	blink	blimp	dumb

Add **ch**, **mp**, **nk** or **bl** to complete the words below.

cla

anket

ba

est

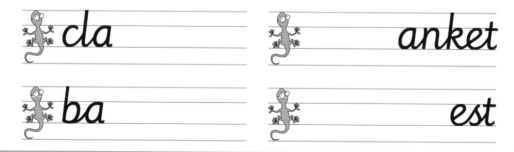

How did you do?

End-low drop-on joins

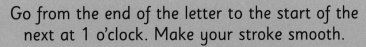

Go from the end of the letter to the start of the next at 1 o'clock. Make your stroke smooth.

Copy the past-tense ending as many times as it will fit.

 ed

Add **ed** to these words to make the past tense.

pick   *need*   *pull*   *point*

Write these verbs in the past tense.

 You might need to change the end of the word first.

tax

gas

fade

add

make

lead

have

sing

How did you do?

End-low drop-on joins

Copy 'Yes yes' and 'No no'.

Remember to use your new style of **e** and **s** in the middle and at the end of words.

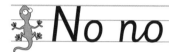 Yes yes

No no

Add a question mark to each question. Answer the question 'Yes' or 'No'.

Don't forget to add a full stop to your answer.

Do you like cheese

Are you a boy

Can you swim

Are you 7 years old

Copy the question. Write your answer.

Is ice made into lead?

How did you do?

End-high horizontal joins

Keep your exit line straight. End your letters on the top body line.

Copy **own** along the line.

 *own*

The **own** has different sounds in different words. Copy the words into sets with the same sound.

| blown | clown | disown | crown | down | drown |
| flown | frown | gown | grown | own | shown |

Sound 1	Sound 2
shown	

How did you do?

End-high horizontal joins

Copy **or** along the lines. Leave a space each time.

Exit the **o** on the top body line and go to the start of **r**. Remember to curl your **r** back up at the end.

 or

Add **or** to these to make new words. Then read them aloud.

doct   *mot*   *tut*   *warri*

Write **or** words to fit the meanings.

                              Someone who acts

                                                 Someone who visits

                              Someone who sails

                                                 A farm vehicle

                              An artist who makes sculptures

                              Someone who writes books

How did you do?

End-high diagonal joins

Finish your letter on the top body line. Then curve up to the start of the next letter.

Practise this join.

wl

Copy these words.

awl   owl

jowls   bowl

drawl   trawler

Add **owl** or **awl** to make words. Then read them aloud.

h   sc   sh   cr

Write the **wl** homophones for the words below. What do they mean?

ball

foul

A homophone is a word that sounds the same but is spelled differently and means something different.

How did you do?

End-high diagonal joins

Make sure the letters don't sit on top of each other.

Practise this join.

wb

Practise these joins with a vowel.

awb

owb

ewb

Match the beginnings and endings.
Then write the compound words.

A compound word is a word made up of two smaller ones.

jaw   berry

straw   ball

snow   bone

How did you do?

End-high drop-on joins

Write these **wa** words next to the words they rhyme with.

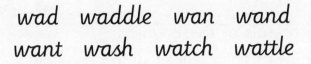

wad   waddle   wan   wand
want   wash   watch   wattle

Finish your letter on the top body line. Then go over to 1 o'clock to start the next letter.

font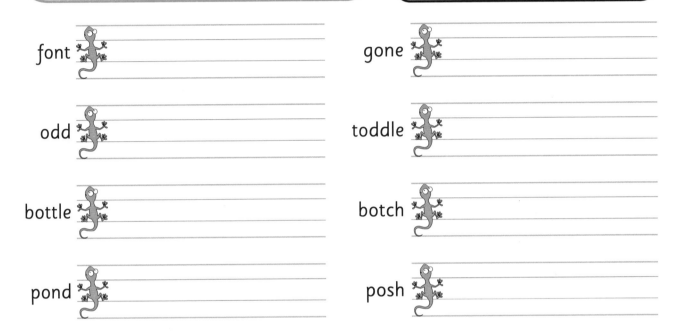

gone

odd

toddle

bottle

botch

pond

posh

Write words with **wa** to match the descriptions.

a stinging insect

a boggy, marshy area

How did you do?

End-high drop-on joins

Remember to use the second style of **s** that starts at 12 o'clock. Don't sit your letters on top of each other.

Join **s** to the last letter to make the plurals of these words.
Write the plurals neatly as many times as they will fit along the lines.

car

cow

pew

satnav

Now write the plurals of these words.

crow

banjo

piano

logo

solo

shampoo

zoo

cuckoo

How did you do?

End-high to e join: re

These words have a tricky join: **r** to **e**. Practise **re**, then copy the words neatly as many times as they will fit.

Draw your **r** exit down to the **e**. Don't let it get too low.

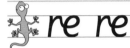 re re

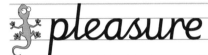 pleasure

 measure

 treasure

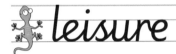 leisure

Complete these words with **ture**.

When words end with **ture**, the **tu** sounds like **ch**.

 fu   frac   na

 cap   punc   vul

 mix   furni   crea

How did you do?

End-high to e join: ve

> End your **v** then bring the stroke down to start **e**. Make sure your letters don't sit on top of each other.

Copy these plurals.

 lives

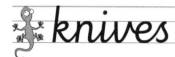 knives

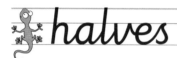 halves

 leaves

Write the plurals.

 elf  shelf

 half  calf

 self  wolf

 loaf  wife

sheaf  thief

How did you do?

Tricky joins: ss

Copy these nouns that end with **ness**.

Finish your **ss** under your joining stroke, not under 12 o'clock. Exit your first **s** along the line you have just drawn.

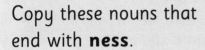 *badness*

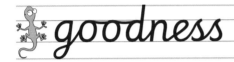 *goodness*

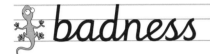 *sickness*

 *deafness*

 *kindness*

Add **ness** to change these adjectives to nouns.

great   *eager*   *fit*

Change the adjectives into nouns using **ness**.

weary    lazy

silly   dizzy

How did you do?

Tricky joins: x

Write the **x** words next to the numbers that match their meanings.

Finish the letter and take your pen to the start of the **x**. Draw the first diagonal then lift your pen to draw the second diagonal.

extra	expel	exam	expect
relax	helix	suffix	prefix

1. _____ You add this to the beginning of a word to change its meaning

2. _____ Take it easy

3. _____ A spiral like a snail's shell

4. _____ You add this to the end of a word to change its meaning

5. _____ A test

6. _____ To send away

7. _____ A bit more

8. _____ Wait for something you know will happen

How did you do?

Revising the joins

Copy this tongue-twister and then try reading it quickly.

Practise all the joins you've learned. Make sure your exit line is smooth.

Reg the Welder wore red wellies when he rode to work in the rain. Reg the Welder rode to the West wearing a really ragged vest.

WEST

 Reg

How did you do?

Back to the past

Write the past-tense verbs in the correct column.

f is a head, body and tail letter.

| rubbed | taped | filed | sloped | tapped |
| cubed | slopped | filled |

Short vowel sound   **Long vowel sound**

Decide if the words are synonyms of 'ran' or 'saw' and write them in the correct column.

Synonyms are words that mean the same thing.

sped   glimpsed   sprinted   spotted   spied   raced

ran   **saw**

How did you do?

Sitting dining

Add **ing** to the words. Then write the new words in the dining room or sitting room based on the spelling rule.

You need to drop the **e** or double the last letter before adding **ing** to these words.

write _____

begin _____

cycle _____

amuse _____

forget _____

invite _____

repel _____

flog _____

Dining room
_____
_____
_____
_____
_____
_____
_____
_____
_____
_____
_____
_____
_____

Sitting room
_____
_____
_____
_____
_____
_____
_____
_____
_____
_____
_____
_____
_____

How did you do?

Weather words

Complete the sentences below by adding **y** to these weather nouns.

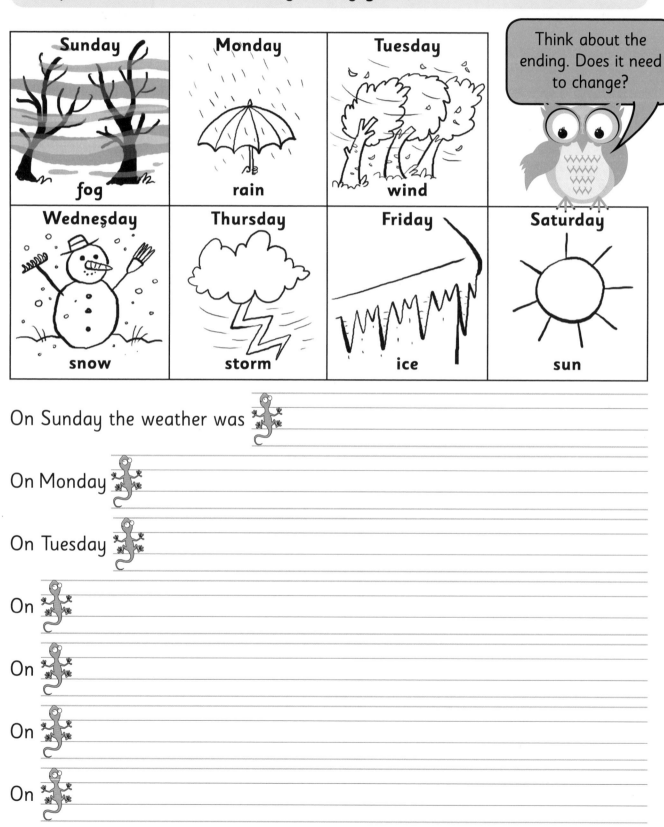

On Sunday the weather was

On Monday

On Tuesday

On

On

On

On

How did you do?

Word addition

Write the plurals of these birds' names.

For plurals that end in **es** you'll need to use the second style of **e** and **s**.

ostrich   chaffinch   thrush

Join a word from the box to one of the words below to create a compound word. Then write its plural.

box   watch   finch   glass

 gold

 letter

 wrist

 hour

How did you do?

Wobbly jellies

Write the plurals of the words on the jellies.

Remember: remove **y** and add **ies**.

party
berry

ruby
pastry

candy
city

country
hobby

_____

_____

_____

Write the plurals of these longer **y** words.

mystery _____

pharmacy _____

pantry _____

strawberry _____

How did you do?

Neatly and tidily

Copy the **ly**. Leave a space each time.

ly

Many adverbs end with **ly**. Copy these adverbs.

neatly   *tidily*   *fully*

Drop onto **e** from **v**.

Add **ly** to form adverbs.

slow   *fair*

even   *wrong*

You may need to change the endings.

Copy the words and add **ly** to form adverbs.

simple   *humble*   *dim*

How did you do?

Less is more

Add **less** to each noun to make an adjective.
Then write the word in full.

less means
without or missing.

aim

need

mind

cord

Write **less** adjectives that mean the same as these phrases.

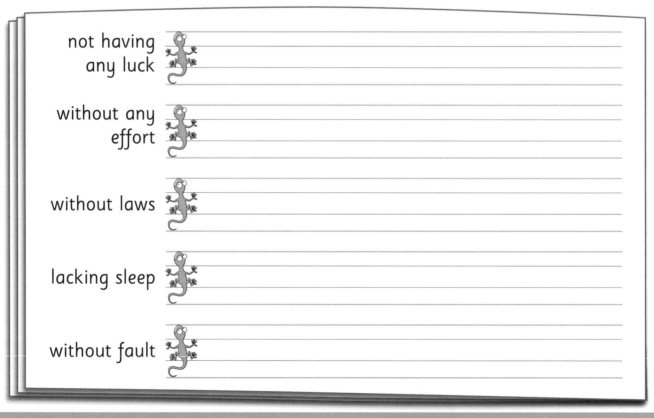

not having
any luck

without any
effort

without laws

lacking sleep

without fault

How did you do?

Full of it

Even though the **ful** suffix means 'full', the suffix has one **l** not two.

Change **less** to **ful** to make an adjective with the opposite meaning.

less	ful
harmless	
powerless	
useless	
colourless	
careless	
cheerless	
hopeless	
painless	

How did you do?

Compare it

Add **er** to each adjective. Then write the words in full to show the motto of the Olympic Games.

We use **er** to compare two things.

 *fast*　　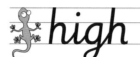 *high*　　 *strong*

Add **er** to these adjectives for a motto for schoolwork, then write it in full.

 *smart*　　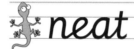 *neat*　　 *tidy*

Write **er** mottoes for these people using adjectives from the box.

Think about the words. Does the ending need to be changed?

| tough | fit | wise | kind | calm | hardy |
| clever | quiet | brave | bold | gentle |

a teacher

a soldier

How did you do?

All the best

We use **est** to compare more than two things.

Add **est** to each adjective. Then write the word in full.

great

small

soon

soft

Add **est** to these adjectives. Just write the word in full.

Remember those endings! Do they need to change?

funny

early

fine

sad

jolly

trim

glum

muddy

How did you do?

A fraction of a word

Write the **tion** nouns from these verbs.

Cross the **t** and dot the **i** at the end.

| act | adopt | protect | prevent |

Add **tion** to these verbs to make nouns.

You will need to change the word endings first.

attend _____

inflate _____

relate _____

create _____

promote _____

illustrate _____

pollute _____

calculate _____

ignite _____

intend _____

How did you do?

Fantastic families

Write the **ic** adjective from each word family.
The first has been done for you.

Remember all letters sit on the writing line and touch the top body line.

word	ic adjective
cube cuboid	*cubic cubic cubic cubic*
acid	
Arab Arabia	
scene scenery	
metre centimetre	
base basement	
history historian	
tragedy	

How did you do?

What do I do?

Write the nouns using **ist** to show what the people do.

The ending **ist** means a person or member.

I play the violin.

violinist

I play the harp.

_____

I play the cello.

_____

I play the organ.

_____

I cycle around.

_____

I go on tours.

_____

I motor along.

_____

How did you do?

It's the opposite

un means the opposite.

Write the opposite of each word using the prefix **un**.

tidy _____

kind _____

likely _____

equal _____

Add **un** to the words in the box and use them in the sentences below.

| even | locked | plug | usual |

The burglar got in through an _____ door.

It is _____ to find an octopus on the beach.

We always _____ the iron after using it.

The road surface was very _____ .

How did you do?

Discover new words

Copy these **dis** verbs.

Remember to use the second style of **s** and end at 12 o'clock. Dot the **i** at the end.

disown

disobey

dislike

disappear

Write the **dis** words in the correct column to show what type of word it is.

 dis means the opposite.

disbelief   disbelieve   distrust   discover   discovery
disobedient   disinfect   dishonest   disloyal

Nouns	Verbs	Adjectives
disbelief	disbelieve	

How did you do?

Repeat it

Practise the **re** join.

Take your pen from the end of **r** to the start of **e**.

 re

Choose a word and add the prefix **re** to complete each sentence.

When we add **re** to a verb, it adds the meaning 'do again' or 'put it back as it was'.

using   set   played   placed   united

Save carrier bags by _____ them.

I enjoyed the DVD so much that I _____ it.

We _____ the carpet with a new one.

When British Summer Time ends we _____ the clocks.

Jack was _____ with his long-lost brother.

How did you do?

Prepare it

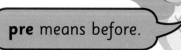

pre means before.

Copy these **pre** words to practise the letters and joins.

preheat

prejudge

Write a **pre** word to match each definition.

prepay   prepare   predict   prevent   prewar

Word	Definition
	Before the war
	Pay in advance
	Get ready before something happens
	Say what is going to happen
	Take action to stop something happening

How did you do?

Deduce it

Copy these **de** words to practise the letters and joins.

de usually shows an opposite action.

depose

demolish

Find these **de** words in a dictionary. Write their meanings.

Make sure your body letters are all the same height.

descend _____

_____

dehydrated _____

_____

deactivate _____

_____

decaffeinate _____

_____

decompose_____

_____

deforest _____

_____

How did you do?

Full of mistakes

Write a **mis** word to match each definition.

mis means wrong.
The words in **bold** type are clues.

treat wrongly

print wrongly

count wrongly

calculate wrongly

direct wrongly

match wrongly

use wrongly

spell wrongly

behave wrongly

How did you do?

Microscopic meanings

Copy the **micro** words.

microbe

microcomputer

microswitch

microorganism

microstructure

microparticle

microworld

microwave

microphone

How did you do?

Mini words

Don't sit the letters on top of each other. Dot the **i** letters at the end.

Copy **mini** as many times as you can.

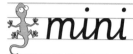 mini

Write a **mini** word from the box to match each definition.

minibus	minicab	minimise	minigolf
minimum	miniaturist	miniskirt	miniature

small bus

to make something smaller

very small

very short skirt

small taxi

small golf game

an artist who paints very small pictures

the smallest amount or lowest level

How did you do?

Auto words

Copy **auto** as many times as you can.

Check your **u** lines are parallel. Form the **o** from 1 o'clock. Cross the **t** at the end.

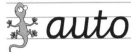 *auto*

Write **auto** words in the gaps so that the sentences make sense.

Auto means 'self'.

autograph   autopilot   automatic   autobiography

A plane is set to fly itself when it is on _____ .

The singer's _____ is called 'My Life in Song'.

I asked him to sign his _____ on it.

Mum doesn't change gear when she's driving.

Her car is an _____ .

 How did you do?

Round and around

Copy these **circ** words twice.

Remember to finish your **r**, then go to where **c** starts at 1 o'clock.

circulation   circular

Copy these sentences.

The prefix **circ** means 'round' or 'around'.

Sir Francis Drake circumnavigated the earth in a ship.

The circumference of a circle is the distance around the edge of it.

How did you do?

From a distance

> The prefix **tele** means 'from a distance'.

Copy **tele**.

 *tele*

Add **tele** to these words.

communication

port   *graph*

vision   *pathy*

scope   *phone*

Write out the words you made.

How did you do?

Transforming words

The prefix **trans** means 'across', 'beyond' or 'through'.

Write these **trans** words.

| transfuse | transfusing | transfusion |
| transformer | transform | transformation |

Write the **trans** words next to their meanings.

transmit   transfer   translate   translucent

Lets some light through

Convert from one language to another

Move or copy from one place or surface to another

Send out a message or television or radio programme

How did you do?

On your bicycle

Write these **bi** words in alphabetical order in the table.

Be careful with joining **r** and **s**.

biplane   bicycle   binoculars   bicentenary   bisect   bilingual

Write the meaning of each word. These clues will help you.

bi means 'two'

ocular means 'about the eyes'

sect means 'to cut or section'

centenary means 'after 100 years'

lingual means 'speaking a language'

Words in alphabetical order	Meanings

How did you do?

On your tricycle

Write the **tri** words in alphabetical order in the table.
Then write the meaning of each word from this list.

Dot the **i** and cross the **t** at the end.

Words

trio	tricycle
trident	triple
tripod	trilingual

Meanings

speaking three languages	three-legged stand
a fork with three teeth	a group of three
a three-wheeled cycle	three times

tri means three.

Words in alphabetical order	Meanings

How did you do?

Pieces of eight

oct means eight!

Copy the words.

 octagon

octogenarian

octave

octet

octopus

octahedron

Look up 'octahedron' and write its meaning.

Tough stuff

Practise the letters and joins in **ough**.
Write **ough** as many times as it fits along the line.

Keep your **o** exit horizontal.

 *ough*

Write the words in sets that rhyme. There are seven sets in total.
Some have been done for you.

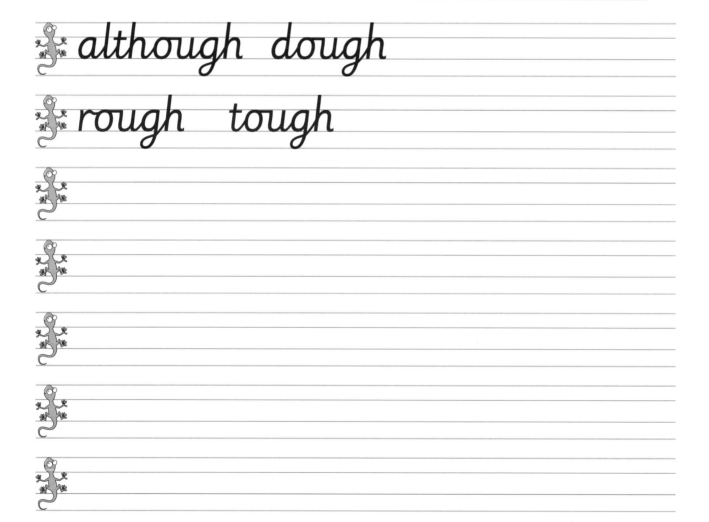

although bough cough dough enough hiccough plough
rough though thorough through tough trough

although dough

rough   tough

How did you do?

Tough stuff

Write **igh** neatly as many times as it fits along the line.

Exit your **g** on the writing line, then go to the start of **h**. Dot your **i** at the end.

 *igh*

Write **igh** words that match the meanings.

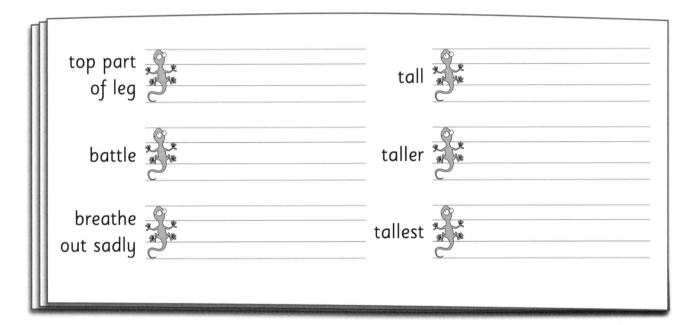

top part of leg

tall

battle

taller

breathe out sadly

tallest

Add these words after 'high' to make compound words. Write them below.

light   chair   jack   land

highlight

All right on the night

Exit your **r** before writing **i**.

Copy these **ight** words.

fight

fright

bright

might

right

sight

slight

tight

Write ten words that begin or end 'light' or 'night'. Some have been done for you.

fortnight headlight nighthawk

How did you do?

Knotty knitting

Keep the circle of your **k** under the top body line.

Practise the letters **kn**.

 kn

Write **kn** words for these definitions. One has been done for you.

A join that you can tie  *knot*

A joint on a finger

The past tense of know

With lumps and bumps

Making things using needles and wool

On your knees

If a word begins with **kn** the **k** is silent.

Hit or bumped

Something you use to cut up your food

How did you do?

In doubt

Many words have a silent **b**.

Copy **mb** and **bt** as many times as they fit.

mb

bt

Read the words aloud then copy them.

tomb   jamb   bomb

debt   doubt   lamb

thumbnail   plumber

A prefix is a group of letters added to the beginning of words and suffixes are letters added to the end.

Add different prefixes or suffixes to make new words. One has been done for you.

bomb **bombed**   climb

doubt   comb

How did you do?

Write it right

Remember to exit **w** and **r** at the top body line, then go to where the next letter starts.

Copy the following.

wra

wre

wri

wro

wru

wry

Write the words that match the definitions.

In many words the **r** sound is spelled **wr**. You don't hear the **w**.

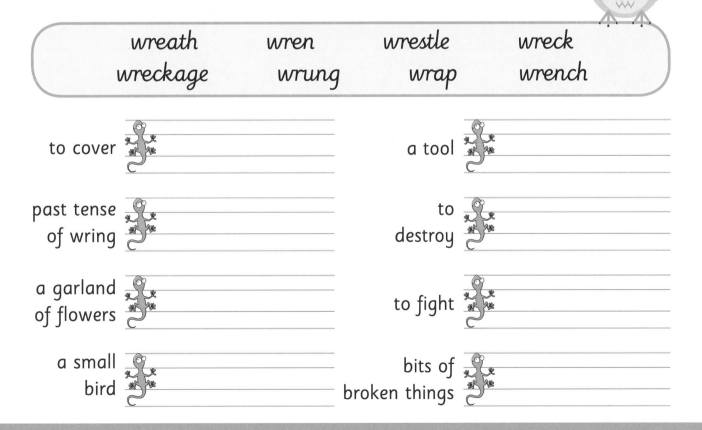

wreath   wren   wrestle   wreck
wreckage   wrung   wrap   wrench

to cover _____

a tool _____

past tense of wring _____

to destroy _____

a garland of flowers _____

to fight _____

a small bird _____

bits of broken things _____

How did you do?

Pronoun addition

A pronoun can be used instead of a noun.

Write the missing pronouns. Two have been done for you.

we   they   their   ours   theirs   our   us
theirs   they   their   we   they

I + you = we

he + she = they

he + it =

me + you =

she + it =

we + you =

his + her =

its + his =

its + hers =

mine + yours =

his + mine =

his + hers =

Write your own sentences using these pronouns.

her

our

How did you do?

Every which way

Copy these words.

Remember the **t** is taller than the top body line but shorter than the head line. Cross it at the end.

this

that

these

those

which

what

Use the words above to complete the sentences. Make sure the sentences make sense.

Which _____ way are you going? I am going _____ way.

_____ time is it? It is time for _____ programme.

_____ programme? The one about _____ author.

Please pass me _____ books. Those books are yours,

but _____ books are mine.

How did you do?

Selfish pronouns

Remember to use the 1 o'clock **s** at the start of words and 12 o'clock **s** in the middle or at the end.

Copy the word on the line.

 self

Write the **self** pronoun to match each of these. The first one has been done.

himself   herself   itself   yourselves
themselves   ourselves   yourself   myself

him   himself

you

me

her

it

us

them

you

Write a sentence using 'myself'.

How did you do?

Sounds the same

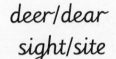

Homophones are words that sound the same but have different spellings.

Write the correct word under each picture.

deer/dear   bear/bare   rode/road   steak/stake
sight/site   sent/scent   sail/sale   stairs/stares

Underline the homophones then write the correct spellings.

Jim gave a loud grown as he fell.

Luckily he didn't brake any bones.

How did you do?

Homophone detective

Underline the homophones that are wrong. Rewrite the homophones with the correct spellings and your favourite sentence from the story.

Amy through the bawl to Raj. He court it but the next time he mist. It went strait threw the window. Unfortunately the window was closed. Amy new it would brake and she was write. A big pain of glass smashed into tiny peaces. "Wheel have to pay for that," she thought.

How did you do?

Homophone choice

Choose the correct homophone. Write the sentences correctly.

Nobody could understand today's maths except/accept Leanne.

Punishments had no affect/effect on Lara's behaviour.

Mum gives us housework to do if we say we're board/bored.

We went for a slay/sleigh ride in the snow.

How did you do?

Shorten it

Copy these words. Don't forget the apostrophes.

Draw the apostrophe at the end from the head line to the top body line.

wouldn't   *shouldn't*   *weren't*   *haven't*   *wasn't*   *mustn't*

 wouldn't

Underline any pairs of words that can be joined and shortened with **n't**. Write the words in the box below.

1. The car will not start.

2. He could not go to the football match.

3. We shall not have time to go to the fair.

4. Dogs are not allowed in the cafe.

5. It does not matter how much it costs.

6. Mum would not let me go out with my friends.

1. _____   2. _____   3. _____

4. _____   5. _____   6. _____

How did you do?

The long and short of it

Practise the letters and joins in these contractions.

Remember to leave a space and write the apostrophe at the end.

I'll

I'd

we'll

we'd

he'll

who'll

Write these as contractions with an apostrophe.

who would _____

you had _____

we would _____

he had _____

they had _____

it would _____

there had _____

it will _____

they will _____

I had _____

I shall _____

there will _____

she will _____

you would _____

How did you do?

In short

Practise the letters and joins in these contractions.

r, v and w are end-high letters.

I've

you've

we've

I'm

you're

we're

Use the words above to complete the sentences. Use each word once.

On my plate is the biggest pizza _____ ever seen.

_____ not joking. It is huge! We all got the same.

_____ taken photos of them and _____ all taking

home enough pizza to last a month! Come and see mine!

_____ got to see this!

_____ not going to believe it until you see it!

How did you do?

Even downstrokes

Copy the words twice.

Make sure your downstrokes are parallel like the example, so they look neat.

Even	Uneven
address ✓	address ✗

believe _____

business _____

describe _____

experiment _____

favourite _____

guard _____

important _____

island _____

library _____

How did you do?

Betty Botter's butter

Copy the tongue twister. Then try saying it very quickly!

Make sure the downstrokes are evenly slanted.

Betty Botter bought some butter,
But, she said, the butter's bitter;
If I put that in my batter
It will make my batter bitter,
But a bit of better butter,
That would make my batter better.
So she bought a bit of butter
Better than her bitter butter
And she put it in her batter
And the batter was not bitter.

How did you do?

Car to the star

Circle the mistakes in the limerick.

Joins? Size? Space? Shape? Slant?

There was a young Man with a car,

People said that he'd go far.

The people were right

On Saturday night

He drove it up to a star.

Now write the text correctly.

How did you do?

Enlarge it

Copy the newspaper titles to fill the spaces on the newspapers on this page and page 67.

Never join your capitals.

1. The Toytown Clarion   **2.** The Children's Gazette

3. The Narnia Express   **4.** The Hogwart's Echo

5. The Sleepy Hollow Times   **6.** The Teletubbies Mirror

7. The Grub Street Journal   **8.** The Dalek News

1.

2.

3.

How did you do?

4.

_____

5.

_____

6.

_____

7.

_____

8.

_____

How did you do?

Shrink it

Make sure your writing is the correct size for this postcard.

Copy the greeting and the beginning of the message on to the postcard. Finish the sentence and write two more. Sign off saying who it is from. On the right, write the name and address of the person you're writing to.

Dear Lena,

We're having a great time in...

POSTCARD

How did you do?

Grow and shrink

These words grow or shrink with the lines.
Copy these to shrink or grow in the same way.

Practise writing in different sizes. What do you prefer?

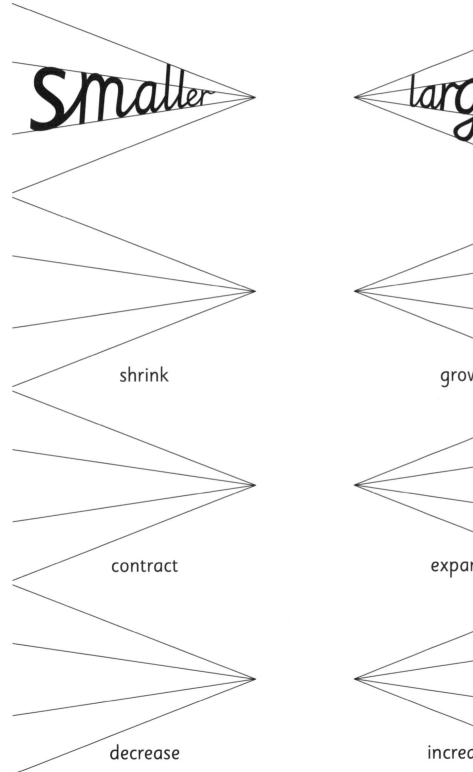

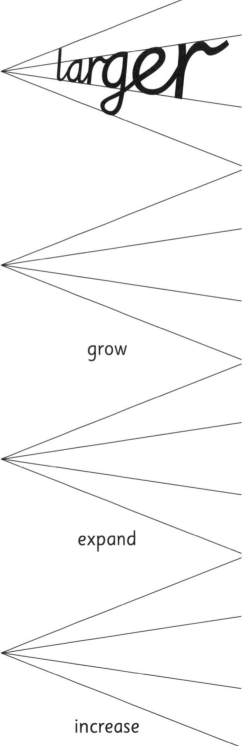

shrink

grow

contract

expand

decrease

increase

How did you do?

Knock, knock

Copy the sentences and add the correct punctuation marks.

Make sure the dots of the punctuation marks sit on the writing line.

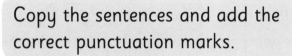

Knock, knock

Who's there

It's Harry

Harry who

Harry up, it's cold out here

Write another 'Knock, knock' joke you know.

How did you do?

Poem

Copy the poem, taking care to place the commas correctly on the lines. You could sing it, if you like!

Start at the writing line and draw your comma down.

Head, shoulders, knees and toes,
Knees and toes.
Head, shoulders, knees and toes,
Knees and toes.

And eyes, and ears, and mouth,
And nose.
Head, shoulders, knees and toes,
Knees and toes.

Oranges and lemons

Copy the sentences and put in the inverted commas.

Ask your teacher which inverted comma to use – double or single.

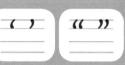

Oranges and lemons, said the bells of Saint Clements.
You owe me five farthings, said the bells of Saint Martins.
When will you pay me? said the bells of Old Bailey.
When I grow rich, said the bells of Shoreditch.
When will that be? said the bells of Stepney.
I do not know, said the great bell of Bow.

How did you do?

Let's grow a sentence

Copy each sentence as neatly as you can.

The cat watched.

The cat watched the bird.

All morning the cat watched the bird.

All morning the cat watched the bird and waited.

Make sure your body, head and tail letters are all the same heights.

Continue to grow the sentence.

How did you do?

Practise pangrams

Pangrams are sentences that contain all the letters of the alphabet.

Copy the sentences neatly.

Pick by hand twelve extra juicy lemons for squeezing.

Heavy boxers perform quick waltzes and jigs.

A wizard's job is to vex chumps in fog.

Pack my box with five dozen liquorice allsorts in jugs.

All five questions asked by experts amazed the watching judges.

How did you do?

Note it well

Read the passage below and then cover it with a piece of paper.
On the note pad, make notes about what you remember.

Do not use full sentences when you make notes.

Camels have ways of surviving in a desert:
- They can close their nostrils to keep out the sand and their long eyelashes keep it out of their eyes. Patches of leathery skin on their knees help to stop hot sand burning them when they lie down to rest.
- Their big, wide hooves help them to walk on soft sand.
- Their tough mouths let them eat the spiky, tough plants that grow in deserts.
- They store fat in their humps. They can convert this to water when they need it.

Your note-taking style will be messier, but it still needs to be readable.

How did you do?

Write a story

Continue this story.

Creative writing doesn't need to be neat. You can write it neatly when you edit.

Beth and Jack often sat on the wall outside Beth's house. They watched everyone. One day a van stopped outside number 14. The driver got out.

"There's no point in ringing the bell," said Jack to Beth. "They went away on Saturday and they're not coming back until next week. Shall we tell him?"

"No," said Beth. "We don't know who he is. He might be a burglar."

So they watched. The man called from the door and another man got out of the van. They went into the house.

"Maybe they're back," said Jack. Beth didn't think so because she didn't see anyone answer the door, although it was open.

_____

_____

_____

_____

_____

_____

_____

_____

How did you do?

Write a poem

Continue this poem about how animals move. It doesn't have to rhyme, but you could use some rhyme or alliteration if you like.
Make each verse seem like the animal moving.

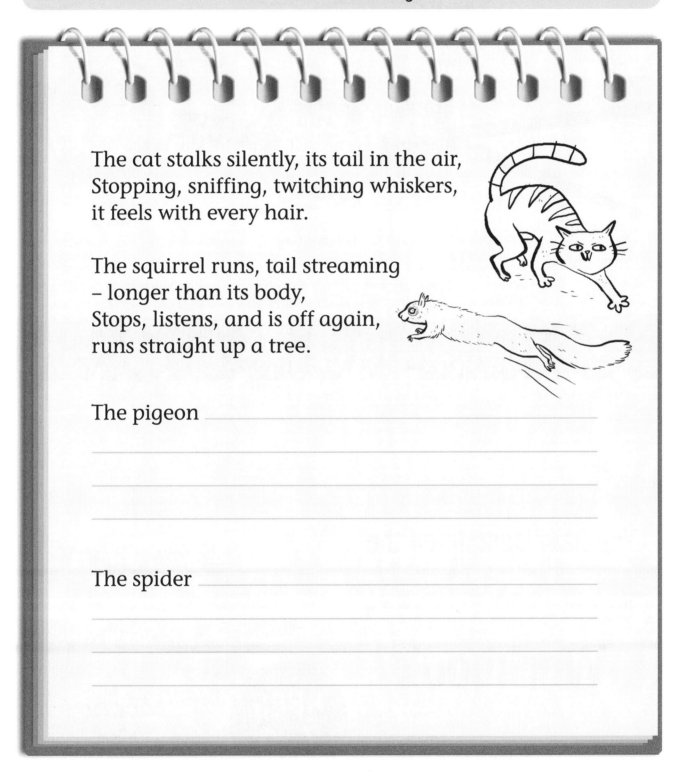

The cat stalks silently, its tail in the air,
Stopping, sniffing, twitching whiskers,
it feels with every hair.

The squirrel runs, tail streaming
– longer than its body,
Stops, listens, and is off again,
runs straight up a tree.

The pigeon _____

_____

_____

_____

The spider _____

_____

_____

How did you do?

Progress chart

Colour in Ollie when you have completed the chapter.

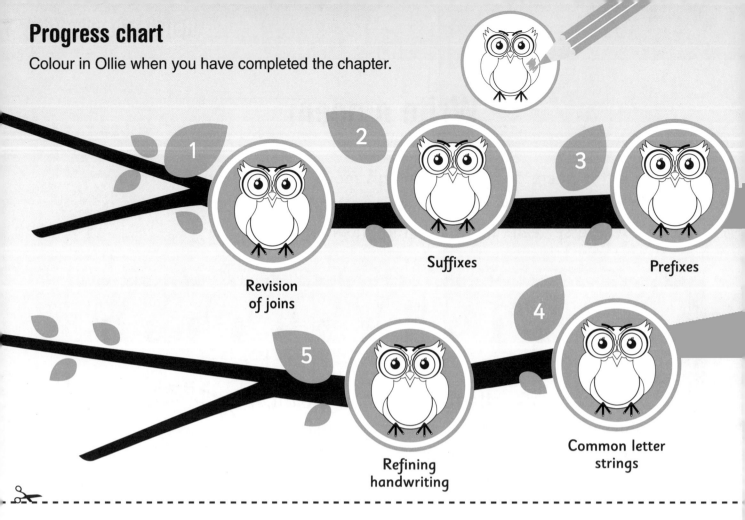

1 Revision of joins

2 Suffixes

3 Prefixes

4 Common letter strings

5 Refining handwriting

CONGRATULATIONS!

Name: ....

You have completed the
Handwriting
Workbook

AGES
7–9

Age: ....   **Date:** ....